POEMS

FOR YOUR
Pandemic

D1432307

GARY ALEXANDER

outskirts
press

Outskirts Press, Inc.
http://www.outskirtspress.com

Paperback ISBN: 978-1-9772-3872-6
Hardback ISBN: 978-1-9772-3875-7

Library of Congress Control Number: 2021901998

Cover & interior illustrations © 2021 Kasidy Sinteral Scott. All rights reserved - used with permission.
Interior images © 2021 pixabay & vecteezy.com. All rights reserved - used with permission.

Outskirts Press and the "OP" logo are trademarks belonging to Outskirts Press, Inc.

PRINTED IN THE UNITED STATES OF AMERICA

CONTENTS

ACKNOWLEDGEMENTS

There is no way I could have written anything, or actually made it through this strange year without the companionship and support of my wife, Anita. When two adults are locked down for an entire year together it requires special patience and understanding. Fortunately, she had a lot of both. While I regretted her choice to sleep in another bedroom (in our house), I knew there would be no middle of the night poetry writing if she had stayed. As you will read in some of the poems, Anita was my "pandemic partner," 24/7 during this Covid-19 year.

I want to also thank my sister, Gail Alexander Wise, for her proof reading, and suggestions that led to revisions, and more readable poems. She is my only sibling and shares my genes in so many ways - addicted to history, ice cream, and politics just to name a few.

Finally, Sandria (Sandie) Turner deserves much more than just thanks and credit. As my lifelong legal secretary, she has been able to pump out legal briefs, agreements, emails, and work recently on drafts and edits of poetry. You would never believe the process we now use with me in Florida, and Sandie in Maryland; but somehow it still works after more than 50 years working together.

My Publishing Assistant, Deni Sinteral-Scott, held my hand through the process and was very helpful. Most of the illustrations were done by Kasidy Sinteral-Scott (yes, they are a mother/daughter Team), and she helped create just the right "look" for my poems. I must add that they were both supportive of the idea for a humorous look at how we lived and tried to cope with 2020 - a year we are thankful has ended. I tried many times to stop the whole process, but they wouldn't let me!

INTRODUCTION

As 2020 began, and January rolled into February, none of us were prepared for the public health crisis that was coming. I know I wasn't. The Covid-19 Virus Pandemic would soon dominate our lives for the rest of the year. Some parts of the country were hit harder than others and suffered at different times as the virus spread. The news was dominated with virus statistics - growing numbers of people infected, people on ventilators, and rising death tolls. Unemployment skyrocketed, as the economy faltered, and working from home became universal. We found new ways to communicate — "virtual" was the new normal with Zoom and Facetime. There was a sad, daily long line of cars with families just trying to get food, and then lines of people trying to get tested. Restaurants and businesses closed, entertainment, and travel ended as countries around the world closed their borders to visitors.

The pandemic struck the United States at a time the country was already divided into partisan political camps for the Presidential election coming up in November. Protests, riots, and political demonstrations added stress to our daily routine. Many watched all this with a growing lack of trust given the mixed messages from government, scientists, media, press, and pundits that we heard day and night. Like millions of Americans, I found it difficult to get a decent night's sleep.

Somehow, and for some reason, I began writing poems -nothing fancy, just poems about what was happening. I began thinking in rhyme! There I was -at 3 or 4am — writing poems on my iPad, so I could get back to sleep. I found this poetic diversion to be relaxing and enjoyable.

The more I learned about the deadly Spanish Flu pandemic of 1918/19, that killed more than 650,000 Americans, and perhaps fifty million worldwide; I noted amazing similarities with what we were now experiencing with Covid 19. The public health guidelines 100 years ago were strikingly similar to the advice we were now being asked to follow: masks, wash our hands repeatedly, avoid crowds, social distance and more. The battle between individual choice and universal compliance that we see today had its roots just over 100 years ago. Then they were called "mask slackers" who refused the required "muzzled misery" and other government mandates. The "Anti-Maskers League" was formed to fight the regulations in San Francisco which was enforcing fines ($5 to $10) and jail time (10 days).

The good news was that in spite of the enormity of the pandemic (then and now), Americans continue to show their universal sense of humor. There were many examples of poems written in the darkest times of the Spanish Flu that helped to get folks to relax, laugh, and enjoy a light-hearted look at their pandemic. Smithsonian Magazine in its July 2020 issue, quoted from the 1918 poem "The Spanish Flu May Get You, Too!" by James Daniel Boone (See Katherine A. Foss, Zocato Public Square).

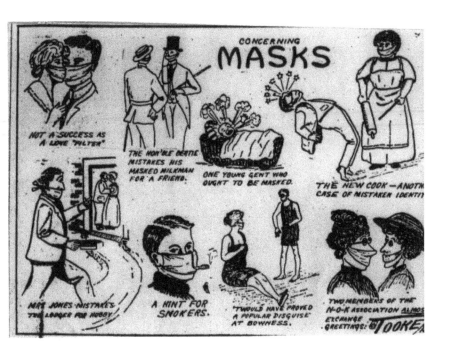

"Oh, we are quarantined, I guess
For 'bout a million years
But if we don't get out of here
We'll burst right out in tears."

We feel much of the same loss now and can share the frustration they felt in their influenza restricted lives. Children's author, Edna Groff Diehl told us in her 1918 poem called "Flu Bound":

"The street crowd surged – but where to go?
The bar? The concert? Movies? No!
Old Influenza's locked the door to Pleasure Land.
Oh, what a bore!"

I stumbled onto an article dated March 26, 2020 called: "The Spanish Flu Poem, 1918" written by Jack Neely, Executive Director of the Knoxville History Project. He described how Knoxville, Tennessee was shut down in October 1918, with movie theaters, pool halls, dance halls, churches, all closed. There were still bond sales underway to support the funding of World War I, and many cities around the country made exceptions to influenza limits on public gatherings to enable large bond rallies. Knoxville waived its public health shutdown by permitting a three-day Liberty Bond drive celebration. Thousands attended and were crowded into a three block stretch of Gay Street from Wall to Church Street. At that time Vine Street was called "Black Broadway" - a long urban street lined with African American businesses. During October 2018, more than 200 Knoxvillians died of the virus!

It is an honor to dedicate this 2020 collection of "Poems for your Pandemic" to Joe Bogle of Knoxville, a black man who lived on Patton Street with his small family; Joe is believed to be the author of the 1918 Spanish Flu Poem. His humor and style inspired me and set the tone for all my sleepless nights writing about our current pandemic. Not much has changed over the last one hundred years, has it?

Americans still have a sense of humor like Joe, even in the face of our biggest challenges. By the end of this strange year, I have not yet gotten the virus, but I do speak in rhymes at lot!

Gary Alexander
December 2020

Contact: alexstrategies@gmail.com

For additional information go to:
www.downtimewithme.com
or
www.outskirtspress.com/poemsforyourpandemic

THE SPANISH FLU POEM, 1918
By: Joe Bogle

"Listen here, children," said Deacon Brown,
There's something new just struck this town,
And it's among the white and the colored, too
And I think they call it the Spanish Flu.

They say it starts right in your head:
You begin to sneeze and your eyes turn red.
You then have a tight feeling in your chest,
And you cough at night and you just can't rest.

Your head feels dizzy when you are on your feet;
You go to your table and you just can't eat.
And if this ever happens to you,
You can just say you got the Spanish Flu.

Now, I got a brother and his name is John,
And he went to buy a Liberty Bond.
And he stopped to hear the big band play,
Upon the corner of Church and Gay.

But when he heard about the Flu-
It tickled me and would tickle you
He bought his bond and went away;
Said he'd hear the band some other day.

But just as he got down on Vine
He began to stagger like he was blind.
And a doctor who was passing by
Said: "What is the matter with this country guy?"
But as soon as he asked John a question or two,
He said: "Good night, you got the Spanish Flu."

When In Quarantine

PEOPLE who are in quarantine are not
isolated if they have a Bell Telephone.

The Bell Service brings cheer and encouragement to
the sick, and is of value in countless other ways.

Friends, whether close at hand or far away, can be
easily reached, because Bell Service is universal service.

THE CENTRAL UNION TELEPHONE CO.

Telephone Building, E. High St.

R. B. HOOVER, Manager / Springfield, Ohio

CORONAVIRUS IN THE U.S.

AS OF MAY 27 2020 5:47PM

TOTAL CASES: **1,705,714**

TOTAL DEATHS: **100,715**

SOURCE: JOHNS HOPKINS UNIVERSITY / NBC NEWS

LIVE
MSNBC
6:50 PM CT

ARE WE DONE WITH YOU YET?

THIS VIRUS IS A HOAX?

This Covid 19 thing wasn't real for all of the folks,
Many believed the pandemic was nothing but a hoax!

No public health guidelines controlling their fate,
Since the CDC and science was really Deep State!

No matter the deaths and infections, and each daily tally,
They were seen in large numbers at a motorcycle rally!

As our country closed down with the virus on fire,
None of this mattered to a closed-minded denier.

They shouted and pouted: "it was all a big trick",
But soon these deniers began to fall sick.

In the end things really got worse,
Those virus deniers were part of our curse!

If you Hate Wearing a Mask,
You're Really not Going to Like
Wearing a Ventilator.

A LITTLE VIRUS HISTORY

There is some virus history I think you should know,
A few have been cured – like yellow fever and polio.
Over the years every so often a virus would appear,
Causing a health issue and a whole lot of fear.

Some kinds of virus seem to come straight from bats,
The Black Plague we think was caused by very bad rats.
Mosquitos caused yellow fever that did get a cure,
Scientists search for clues and they want to be sure.

Swine Flu came from pigs, and they get the blame,
Measles, and Mers, there are so many to name.
Bird flu we know was caused by some birds.
Others are linked to strange kinds of turds!

Spanish Flu wasn't caused by Spaniards you see,
Nothing could stop that virus from breaking free.
Ebola comes from monkeys, don't let this virus spread,
Its deadly outcome could leave many millions dead.

The Aids virus we know now was very complex
Brought on they said by unprotected sex!
Marburg, and Measles and something called Sars,
It's no wonder people spend hours drinking in bars!

A cure by vaccine makes us all celebrate,
But don't let those virus cells ever mutate.
The virus is smart - its ever so clever ...
Let's face it - viruses will be around us forever!

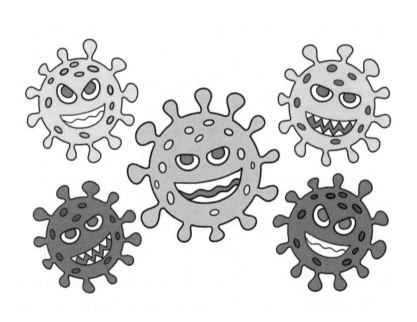

WE WERE SCARED
SHITLESS OF COVID 19

We were scared shitless of Covid 19,
Worst virus any of us had ever seen,
At first we were clueless on what we should do,
So Many folks had it and never, even knew.

As It came and it went - spreading over the lands,
We started washing and washing and washing our hands.
Social distancing they said: "stay six feet apart"
And make sure to spray every grocery cart.

Businesses closing, and curfews in place,
If you got it — your contacts we trace.
Masks were helpful it's the least you could do!
Some still refused - they never had a clue.

Thanksgiving was weird, a feeling of doom,
To see your loved ones, you had to use Zoom!
On and on that virus would spread,
It was shocking just how many were dead.

Too many people now were a mourner,
While Trump lied: "We are rounding the corner."
2020 was the pits, I can't tell you how bad,
But a vaccine is coming and we are so glad!

A year unlike any we had ever seen,
A year of without fun due to Covid 19!

WHY IS TOILET PAPER SO HARD TO FIND?

Of all the things that we now can't find,
Toilet paper would never have come to my mind,
I confess I took toilet paper for granted,
Weren't zillions of toilet paper trees planted?

But alas, store shelves are amazingly bare,
You aren't going to find toilet paper anywhere,
It's not a joke, this is not some hype,
What will we do when its soon time to wipe?

Somehow the virus made people afraid,
They thought toilet paper would stop being made.
Somewhere, some place it's all being stored
Or hoarded by people who think they need more!

How much do we need? How much can we use?
Maybe One roll a week divided by two's?

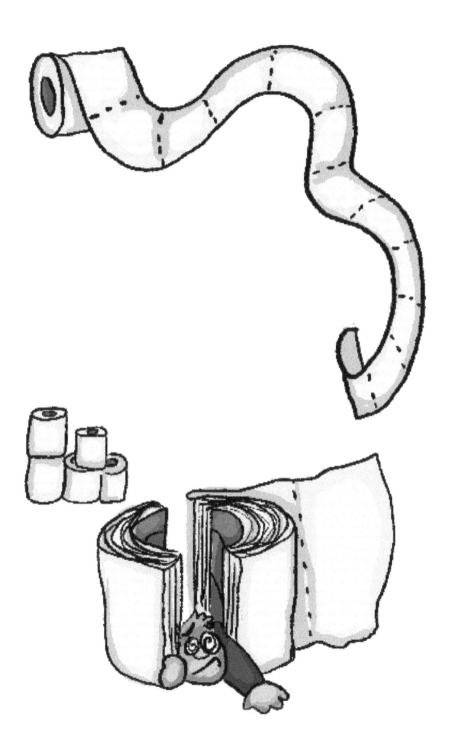

LINE UP, LINE UP, IT'S FOR THE TEST

Line up, line up, it's for the test,
Please drive this way, just like the rest.

Every driver with a look so sour,
Why not - it will take us many an hour!

Just a quick nose swab – it's not even gory,
Results take 6 days that will end your story.

So negative is good, and positive is bad,
The whole process is pretty darn sad.

Pull up sir, keep this line real tight,
Getting tested should not be such a fight!

I'VE LOST MY MASK

I've lost my mask, it must be here?
I've looked high and low and over there.

It fit just right - and never felt clunky
After 5 months, I admit it did smell funky!

It was black and was never too tight,
I could wear it to sleep - it fit just right.

I just keep looking here and there,
Because I wore it everywhere,

Some say masks just come and go,
But I really loved this mask, so…

I guess I will just get another,
Maybe borrow one from my brother.

But it will never, ever be the same,
My mask is gone, I've got no one else to blame!

YOU CAN ZOOM
IN ANY ROOM!

If you can't go to work and you still need to meet,
And seeing your family is a much-needed treat,
Or if you're locked down or shut in with no place to be,
Its ZOOM time right now to hear and to see!

You have to use Zoom - for the kids out of school,
It's hard to believe - our lives are now virtual?
You can Zoom any time and even at night,
Join without video when you don't look quite right!

Your background's a beach - what a virtual surprise,
Or surrounded by books looking ever so wise.
The best way to prove you are really astute,
Say as little as possible, or just stay on mute.

Zoom is our new normal, it's what we all use,
It helps us get rid of our pandemical blues.
If only we knew - Covid came as a shock,
I should have bought shares of Zoom common stock!

WHO IS THIS GREAT GUY FAUCI?

There's a great man named Fauci, so they say,
He's 80 and works a 22-hour day!

A doctor of note on infectious diseases,
A principled guy who won't stand for sleazes.

He worked on Aids, Ebola, Sars and Mers,
And kept all of them from getting worse.

He gives straight advice for every task,
And would never be seen without wearing a mask.

Known as a man telling us just like it is,
Always one step ahead is this medical whiz.

Having him on duty in this Covid year,
Helped calm our country of the virus we fear.

Thank you dear Fauci for all you have done,
With Kudos for all the virus wars you have won!

OUR PANDEMIC AIR FRYER

Stuck in the house and cooking much more,
Afraid of the Covid outside our front door!
So, what can we cook or what can we get?
We want a new gadget not a new pet!

To cook with less fat, and healthier too,
In a pandemic that's the smart thing to do.
We need to cook fast, and try to eat smart,
But not just food that is good for our heart.

We called a few friends, and emailed some more,
What could we buy, we can't get to a store!
So tell us dear friends what did you acquire?
Their answer was clear - "GO buy an air fryer"!

In two days we had one from Amazon Prime,
Amazing - now we cook on it most of the time!
Our wings are to die for, fudge brownies are yummy,
The downside for sure is my growing fat tummy.

Think how lucky we are to have this new toy,
One thing during Covid that we really enjoy!

SPRING CLEANING,
ALL YEAR LONG!

Covid locked us down the fastest we've seen...
By April, all we could do is get up and clean.
I'm working inside and out and all over our house,
Under the watchful eye of my hard cleaning spouse!

The Virus was here, there was nothing else to do,
I begged her for helpers, us two was too few.
Each closet, and the shelves in all of the rooms,
With buckets, and rags, we both had our brooms.

No time to waste, or talk, or even to eat,
Why work so hard with no deadline to meet?
It really got tough when we did the garage,
I saw helpers coming, sadly, it was just a mirage.

Where everything went, I had no say,
Most of my stuff she just gave it away.
By the end of the month I was singing her tune,
So we are cleaning again for the whole month of June!

MY WIFE'S A BARBER!

My wife worked in banking until she retired,
Taking care of me and our house now - she's really wired.
Five grandkids, and a big family of kin,
Finding out she could Barber was sure a big win!

This year was Covid, so we were trapped in our house,
Who knew my hair could be cut by my talented spouse?
My hair didn't care it kept growing like crazy,
And my personal grooming had become quite lazy.

To my rescue she came - this Barber in hiding,
With scissors, and clippers my wife came a riding.
So every six weeks while I sat naked in a chair,
She clipped and she buzzed working hard on my hair.

She trimmed, and she shaved, going clip, clip, clip
And the whole thing was cheaper, she refused every tip!
Cleanup was tricky, white hair all around,
She vacuumed me all over - lord what a sound!

Each haircut she did made me cry out so loud:
"My wife's my barber - boy am I proud!"

LYSOL, CLOROX,
AND PURELL,
...OH MY...

Lysol, Clorox, and Purell, oh my!
So hard to find and forget trying to buy.

We took them for granted for so many years,
Then along came that Covid and stoked up our fears.

Be careful of buying a substitute cleaner,
That Lysol and the others are a whole lot meaner.

I yearn for Purell in the teeny, small size,
A dozen of them now would be quite a nice prize!

Somewhere there are places with products galore,
I'm betting hoarders in China have got a lot more.

So we're using some knockoffs that just aren't much good,
They're on the shelves where Lysol, Clorox and Purell
once stood!

ON ANY GIVEN TUESDAY?

For sports the objective is keeping the virus away,
The NBA played in a bubble – it's a challenge each day.

Football infections are tougher - think of the huddle,
And the NFL schedule has become such a muddle!

Sick players must quarantine for maybe a week,
So the League has to give the calendar one more tweak.

Now we have football, on Tuesday, some games not at all,
The virus controls the schedule all through this fall.

There are no fans in the stands, but we're glued to the screen,
Those refs in their masks are the strangest sights seen!

The playoffs are coming, and the Super Bowl fans crave,
But the coaches and players they all need to behave!

So football goes on, with quarterbacks or not,
This crazy Covid season will never be forgot!

I STREAM, YOU STREAM, WE ALL STREAM...

The pandemic changed how we did lots of things,
It's the downtime and boredom a virus brings.
TV - always important to us played a new role,
We watched many more hours - it all took a toll.

How we watched changed in a brand new way,
It's called "streaming" lasting hours most of your day.
Just find a TV series that lasted for years,
The more episodes the better - something like Cheers!

"Streaming" is watching, and watching some more,
Matters not that you've seen all of it before.
Your choices are endless, with so many carriers,
The FCC has removed all their barriers.

Netflix and Apple, Peacock, Acorn, and Prime,
Pandemic streaming can waste all of your time!
Spend a weekend with a series filmed over twenty years,
At the end of 346 shows -trust me- you will shed tears!

Tears for the actors, and all the plots you've tasted,
Tears for streaming away all the time you've wasted!

PANDEMIC GOLF

By March 2020 came guidelines from CDC,
New golf rules big time for you and for me.
Touching the flag stick was now a big no no,
One person to a golf cart was the new way to go.

No raking the bunkers, no ball washers found,
No food service, or water anywhere around.
Bring your own stuff, a small cooler works nice,
Don't forget, you can't get any ice.

And No one can help you carry your bag,
Mine weighs a ton, makes my muscles to sag.
Stay six feet apart, and away from the hole,
It sure would be easier to just go and bowl!

But golf is our life, and we struggle each round
To hit that little ball straight off the ground.
You still have to putt that ball in the cup,
Covid rules aren't making our handicaps go up!

FATTENING THE CURVE

The Surgeon General just warned of a new health threat,
Pandemic Obesity is here and its bad you can bet!
It's all over-hitting the North and the South,
Americans just putting too much food in their mouth,

We are causing a brand new health crisis,
By eating more pizza, and apple pie slices.
And donuts, and candy, and fried foods too much,
Eating all of the fattening foods we can touch.

We've tripled our intake of things like ice cream,
And crave nothing but comfort foods- so it would seem,
So with nothing to do, and nowhere to go,
Our American fat has started to grow!

We must try and cut back before it's too late,
Not a fat moment to lose, start now- please don't wait!
With the toilet paper shortage we hit a new low,
Because the more we eat, the more we will go!

So, get up, get out, live in a physical way,
Make the goal: Do your ten thousand steps a day!
Help make Pandemic Obesity no more of a threat,
Then we can go back to just being obese you can bet!

HAVE YOU SEEN THE NEW VACCINE?

They say it's coming this new vaccine...
The toughest one we've ever seen.
Its stored in frozen secret racks,
Just two shots stops Covid in its tracks!

Virus studies have made us wiser,
The first one out is made by Pfizer.
All of us can get it, at no cost - its free,
And us old folks will have high priority.

Some don't trust vaccines at all,
They don't get flu shots every fall.
They say this Covid vaccine passed every test
This one is safe it's the very best.

Just get the shot in your community,
No more Covid – they have herd immunity!
Its 94% effective, which sounds pretty good,
Go ahead, you get it first? I think you should!

EVEN SANTA MUST FOLLOW CDC GUIDELINES

Everything is different this year, there's so many flaws,
Lots of changes, really - even for Santa Claus.
Yes, this pandemic affects jolly old St Nick,
The CDC warns: "Kids will make Santa sick!"

Sadly, Covid guidelines also apply to his elves,
They can't come close either, we're protecting ourselves.
So, no pictures with Santa, no kids on his lap,
And no Santa sleigh flying all over the map!

All Santa's reindeer are penned up in one state,
Grounded until this virus finally starts to abate.
But what to our wondering eyes will appear?
Santa's on Zoom with reception so clear.

Or Facetiming children to make sure they're glad,
Making 2020 the best Christmas kids ever had!
(Message rates will apply and there will be a charge
Thirty-five dollars for six minutes of Santa seems a bit
large!)

TWO PEOPLE FOR CHRISTMAS?

Two people for Christmas – it's just you and me?
Hard to believe that's all there will be,
No grandkids, no children, and no family?
Why are we killing ourselves trimming a tree?

We both are dressed up, but not very formal,
Sadly, nothing these days seems to be very normal!
Our pies are baking, we made cookies galore,
We should have just gone to the grocery store!

We've hung stockings, and done so much more,
We have two big wreaths outside our front door!
And lights shine everywhere both inside and out,
We want to be happy, to laugh and to shout!

It's the virus that's keeping our people away,
With Covid their traveling is not A-OK.
This whole year has just been a pain,
Flattening the curve is making us insane!

Hanukah, and Kwanza they weren't the same,
But it's nobody's fault, give Covid the blame!
Just me and my wife 24/7 every day,
It's getting quite hard to think of new things to say.

We're tired doing holidays in this whole new way,
So we're holding Christmas again - probably next May!

THERE WAS A TIME...

There was a time I held my head high,
And looked straight at folks — eye to eye.
So many ways I could show my pride,
In country, family, friends on each other's side.
I took for granted that others cared
About the poor, the sick, and those so scared.

There was a time we could argue back and forth,
Didn't matter you were from east, south, west, or north.
We could read the news and believe it was true,
And watch anything with friends whether old or new.
Never worried that I judged them, or they judged me
For supporting a President, a Party, or some policy.

There was a time before cable news,
When conspiracy theories weren't our daily views.
We had leaders with plans who inspired our youth,
Leaders we trusted for speaking the truth.
Where we lived wasn't counted by "red" or by "blue",
Our country was respected in a worldwide view!

There was a time we read books, and loved history,
Before Facebook we used our eyes to "see".
When research was fun, and helped us to think,
No answer by Google, before you could blink!
We spoke words to each other, and heard what was said,
Not by twitter, or text, where our language is dead!

By the first week in January 2021, Covid-19 infections in the United States totaled more than 20 million, and deaths had reached a staggering 353,000 Americans. There was a feeling of hope with newly approved vaccines being rolled out. The long lines of people trying to get food, or be tested, had morphed into new lines of people – mostly senior citizens, trying to get the vaccine. There are now reports that the Covid-19 virus was mutating and changing and becoming more infectious. It has been, and still is a very unsettling time. The Covid 19 virus has disrupted our lives, and things are still worrisome, and unpredictable. Guidelines are constantly changing. Many have survived an infection, but too many mourn family and friends they have lost.

As we move into 2021, everyone is hopeful the new vaccines will help slow and eventually stop the Covid-19 Virus. Most have trusted science, and are hopeful for the chance to be vaccinated, but there are still so many unanswered questions. While our lives were turned upside down, my wife and I know how fortunate we were not to be sick, hungry or mourn a family member. With no traveling we haven't seen two of our five grandkids (Max and Maya) for more than a year, and this will be our priority to fix in 2021. Its just hard to relax, and shake off the effects of this unexpected, and challenging 2020 year ---- isn"t it?

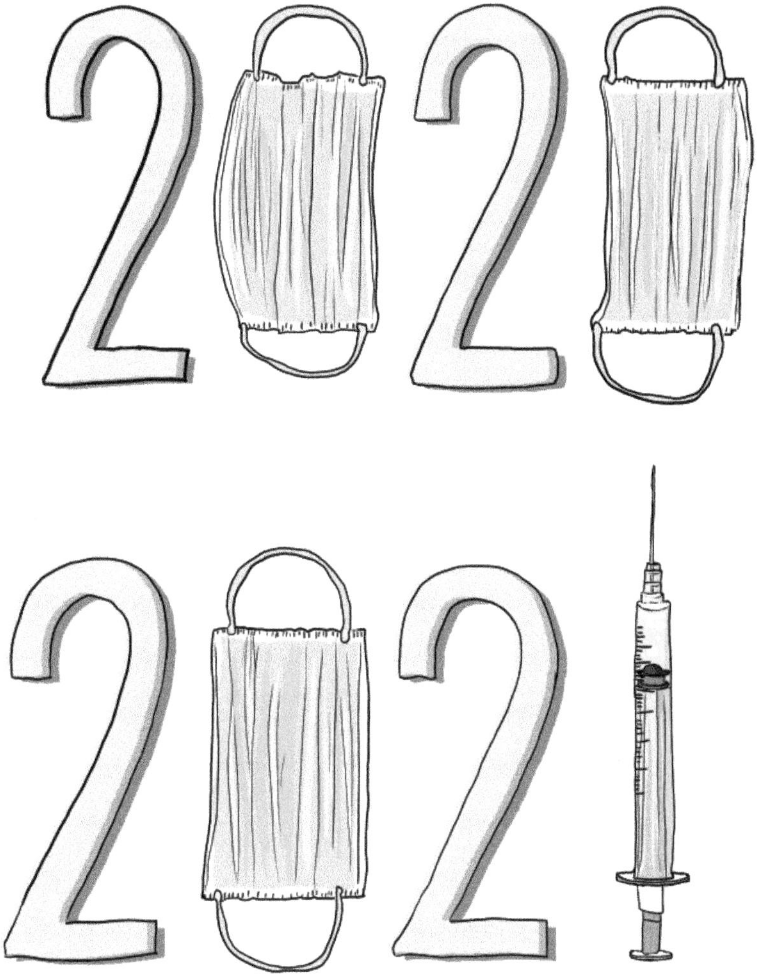

CPSIA information can be obtained
at www.ICGtesting.com
Printed in the USA
BVHW061334060421
604325BV00013B/1371